The Glad Cow Cookbook

SUMMER KEIGHTLEY

Graphic Design and Layout by Chad Miller / Fourteen Little Men, Inc.

Published by Glad Cow 2175 Rogers Ln NW Salem, OR 97304

ISBN: 0-9742180-1-4

Printed in Canada

ABOUT THE AUTHOR

Summer Keightley has been vegan for 5 years. She has always had a healthy interest in cooking and baking, which led to her running a home-based vegan baking business for 2 years, Glad Cow Baking. While running her business, she served many local coffee shops and private customers. Glad Cow Baking helped her to learn a lot about how to streamline recipes for ease of use. Summer loves to create recipes that are easy and delicious. She is especially interested in veganizing classic American recipes. Summer lives in Salem, Oregon with her husband and two children in a happy all-veggie household.

ACKNOWLEDGEMENTS

So many people have encouraged me on my book adventure, and I am thankful for everyone's generosity and kindness.

Thank you to Julie for being one of my many recipe guinea pigs and always making my hummus for your parties; I'm so grateful for your friendship. Thank you to Dany for always being willing to eat what I make and testing my recipes in your own kitchen; your tastebuds rock! Thank you, especially, to Elaine; not just for testing my recipes but, more importantly, baking for me in the early days. Thank you to my nephew Tommy for saying that he would actually buy one of my books and meaning it when I thought he was just kidding. Thank you to Colleen, Melissa, and Nicole for always trying my crazy vegan food so bravely! Thank you to Ellen and John for being so supportive of my business. Thank you to Winter and Ruby for believing in me and for your understanding. Thank you to Chad and Emiko for your offers of help when I really, really needed it. Thank you to Jill for your mad editing skills and much needed sanity-saving conversations.

Of course, I could not have done this without my family, who eat what I cook and then tell me exactly what they think: "More mushrooms!" "Why did you choose cumin?" Your honesty was my greatest inspiration. Thank you to my Mom and Dad for never telling me that I have to eat meat in order to survive and for being so normal about my vegan-ness. Thank you to Simon for singing the "McDonald's...ba da ba ba ba...I'm not really lovin' it" song. Thank you to Sarina for sitting on the counter and talking to me while I cook. And last, but certainly not least, an extra big thanks and many, many hugs to Stan for suggesting this book, supporting me and telling me I should spend the next month going to the park to swing and think about life. I love you!

The Way
I Do It

Whenever anyone asks my advice about how to prepare a certain food, I often preface my reply with, "The way I do it is…" I say it this way because I don't want to sound like my way is the only way; I want people to be open and able to explore other options. But, the truth is, I think it is the best way. After all, I cook a lot. It's what I do. Plus, the many, many hours I spend watching the Food Network have to count for something.

USING TOFU

Firm Tofu

Use firm tofu where you would normally use meat or to add texture to other vegan dishes.

Firm tofu acts like a sponge, absorbing – and consequently, taking on the flavor of – any liquid it comes into contact with. For maximum flavor, then, you'll want to start with a fairly dry tofu base. Because tofu comes packaged in water, you'll need to "press" out the liquid before using the tofu. My favorite method (the way I do it) requires some advanced planning, but it's flexible, and easy, too.

To prepare firm tofu:

1. Drain the water from the package

2. Take the block of tofu out of the package and wrap it in a clean, dry kitchen towel.

3. Refrigerate for at least one hour, but up to three days, changing the towel when it becomes saturated.

4. Your tofu is now ready for marinade. The longer you marinade, the more flavorful it will be.

Silken or Soft Tofu

Use blended silken tofu in desserts or as a soup thickener.

To prepare silken tofu:

1. Open the package. There is usually no water to drain.

2. Put the tofu in a blender or food processor.

3. Blend until smooth.

Once it is smooth, you can add it to soup for creaminess, or use as a base for a fruit smoothie (just add fruit and milk), it also makes a dynamite pudding. Blend with sugar, flavoring (vanilla extract, cocoa powder, etc.) and a pinch of salt. Voila! Dessert.

REPLACING EGGS

There are a variety of methods for replacing eggs in my recipes, depending on the desired purpose – adding structure, leavening, adding moisture and/or emulsification (Combining two or more ingredients that don't usually go together well).

Following is a list of egg replacers that I use and how to use them.

- Ener G – This is a commercial product sold in most grocery stores. Use Ener G Egg Replacer for leavening and adding a small amount of structure. It is best used in "quick bread" type recipes (like muffins), but not in recipes requiring a lot of structure (like brownies or soufflé).

- Flax Seeds – To use flax, blend 1 Tablespoon ground flax with 3 Tablespoons of water until the mixture thickens. Use flax for recipes requiring more structure than the Ener G can give, but needing less leavening. It adds moisture as well. It does not add leavening. Good for pound cake. Not so good on it's own for brownies.

- Tofu – Use ¼ c blended silken tofu for recipes that require emulsification and a lot of structure, but no leavening.

- Applesauce or mashed bananas – These will provide moisture only, so are best used in recipes that already have leavening and structure.

COOKING CREATIVELY

I have spent a great deal of time and effort devoted to cooking, and tend to forget that not everyone is as obsessed with food as I am. For me, food itself is infinitely inspiring. I understand, though, that most people aren't like that and need a little nudge now and then to get out of a cooking rut.

TRY THESE IDEAS:

- Take a classic dish and make it your own by substituting an ingredient or seasoning. For example, try adding chili powder instead of paprika to your vegan potato salad.

- Read about ethnic or regional cooking. There are plenty of books on a variety of cuisines at your local library.

- Explore seasoning themes from a particular cuisine types:
  Mexican – oregano, cumin, cayenne, peppers, onions, cilantro, lime
  Italian – oregano, basil, onion, garlic, olive oil, rosemary, tomato, parsley
  Indian – curry, tumeric, garlic, ginger, coriander, cumin, cilantro
  Asian – soy sauce, ginger, sesame, miso, seaweed

Use your knowledge to create your own personal theme. I, for example, have a particular love for paprika, parsley, cumin, salt, sesame and olive oil. One or more of these go into almost every savory thing I make.

It is also fun to experiment with what ingredients go best with particular seasonings. This is especially true with baking and sweet recipes. For example:

- Bananas – cinnamon, nutmeg, cloves, vanilla

- Apples – cinnamon, vanilla

- Pears – nutmeg, vanilla

- Citrus – vanilla, ginger, salt

- Chocolate – vanilla, almond extract, salt, chili

- Mango – coconut, vanilla, cinnamon

- Berries – citrus, vanilla, cinnamon

I hope this book will help you explore cooking and baking. Please give me feedback about your cooking experiences on my website at www.gladcow.com. Overall, I hope this book will help you find joy in what you create in the kitchen.

Baked Goods

BASIC MUFFINS OR QUICK BREAD

This recipe is a good blueprint for making any custom muffin or quick bread you desire.

1 c whole wheat pastry flour or unbleached white flour	*optional seasonings:*
¾ c rolled oats	½ to 1 t cinnamon
1/3 c sugar	1 t your choice extract (vanilla, almond, mint, etc)
2 t baking powder	1 T fresh citrus zest (orange, lime, lemon)
¼ t salt	½ t powdered ginger or 2 t freshly grated ginger
egg replacer equal to one egg	¼ t nutmeg
¾ c non-dairy milk	¼ t cloves
2 T applesauce	
2 T oil	
¾-1 c fruit, nuts or seeds of your choice	

Preheat oven to 400. In a mixing bowl, combine dry ingredients. Add wet ingredients and stir until moistened. Add your choice of fruit or nuts and fold in. Spoon in to greased muffin tins or greased loaf pan. Put in oven and bake for 20 minutes for muffins or 35-40 minutes for loaf until browned. Let cool 15 minutes for muffins and 1 hour for loaf.

Variation Ideas:

Zucchini Walnut (1/2 c each) with cinnamon, vanilla, powdered ginger, nutmeg, and cloves

Apple Cinnamon (1 c peeled and chopped) with cinnamon

Cranberry Orange Ginger (1 c dried cranberries) with orange zest and fresh ginger

May Contain Nuts (1 c your choice nuts, mixed), almond milk, almond extract, nutmeg

Seedy (1 c your choice seeds, mixed), almond extract, vanilla extract, lemon zest

Fresh Berry (1 c berries) orange and lemon zest, vanilla extract

Coconut Lime (1 c shredded coconut) coconut milk, vanilla extract, lime zest, juice of 1 lime, ¼ t baking soda

BUTTERNUT BRAN MUFFINS

These spicy muffins are a great way to get a yellow vegetable in the morning and get your body on the go (if you know what I mean…)

1 c ww pastry flour	½ c non dairy milk
1 c bran	1½ c cooked, cooled, and peeled
½ c oatmeal	butternut squash
2 ½ t baking powder	½ c sugar
1 t cinnamon	¼ oil or applesauce
½ t salt	½ c walnuts chopped fine
¼ t each nutmeg, cloves, & ginger	1 T candied ginger, diced
egg replacer equal to 1 egg	

Combine wet ingredients and mix well. Add all dry ingredients and mix just until blended. Portion into muffin cups and bake at 400° for 15-20 minutes until cake tester inserted in center comes out clean. Makes 6 jumbo or 12 regular sized muffins.

Variation:

Banana Bran Muffins (Omit butternut squash, spices, and candied ginger) Add 2-3 bananas and 1 T vanilla to wet ingredients and add ¼ t cinnamon and 1/3 c chocolate chips to dry. Prepare and bake as above.

BASIC SCONE RECIPE

This is a blueprint for scones. Add chocolate, nuts, fresh or dried fruit. Yummy!

3 c flour	½ c your choice
½ c sugar	optional:
2 ½ t baking powder	1 t your choice extract (vanilla, almond,
1 t salt	mint, etc)
½ t baking soda	1 t your choice spice
½ c vegan margarine	1 t your choice citrus zest (lemon, lime,
¼ c vegan shortening	orange)
1 c non-dairy milk + 1 t vinegar	

Preheat oven to 425. Put flour, sugar, baking powder, salt, and baking soda, and spices or zest if desired in a bowl. Mix well. Add vegan margarine and shortening and press it in with the tips of your fingers until it resembles coarse crumbs. Add liquid and extract if desired and mix until well blended. Add your choice of fruit, nuts, etc. Press dough into a circle on a sheet pan. Cut into eighths like a pie. Sprinkle with sugar if desired. Bake for 15-18 minutes. Let cool slightly.

APPLE COFFEE CAKE

Filled with wonderful apple slices and cinnamon, this moist cake is sure to please!

Topping:	Cake:
1/3 c ww flour	2 c ww flour
¼ c sugar	2-½ t baking powder
¼ c oatmeal	1 t cinnamon
2 T vegan butter or shortening	½ t salt
½ t cinnamon	1 c non-dairy milk
	½ c sugar
	¼ c applesauce
	egg replacer equal to 1 egg
	2 apples peeled and sliced

Mix ingredients for topping with a pastry blender or fingertips until butter is well incorporated. Set aside. Combine wet ingredients except apples. Mix well. Add dry ingredients and mix until blended. Fold in apples. Pour cake batter into an 8X8in square pan or 10in round pan. Sprinkle on topping and bake at 350° for 40-45 minutes until cake tester inserted in the center comes out clean. Let cool for 10-15 minutes before serving.

BERRY COFFEE CAKE

Use any mixture of fresh berries for this summer delight. The jam ensures a pretty berry swirl even when using hardier fruit like blueberries and cranberries.

Topping:	2 ½ t baking powder
1/3 c ww flour	½ t salt
¼ c sugar	¼ t nutmeg
¼ c oatmeal	1 c non-dairy milk
2 T vegan butter or shortening	½ c sugar
½ t cinnamon	¼ c applesauce
Cake:	egg replacer equal to one egg
2 c ww flour	1 cup fresh berries
	2 T berry jam

Mix ingredients for topping with a pastry blender or fingertips until butter is well incorporated. Set aside. Combine wet ingredients except berries and jam. Mix well. Add dry ingredients and mix until blended. Fold in berries and jam until just swirled. Pour cake batter into an 8X8in square pan or 10in round pan. Sprinkle on topping and bake at 350° for 40-45 minutes.

BANANA NUT COFFEE CAKE

Moist, light, and flavorful.

Topping:
1/3 c ww flour
¼ c sugar
¼ c oatmeal
¼ c walnuts
2 T vegan butter or shortening
½ t cinnamon
Cake:
2 c ww flour

2 ½ t baking powder
½ t salt
¼ t nutmeg
2-3 bananas, mashed
1 c non-dairy milk
½ c sugar
¼ c applesauce
egg replacer equal to one egg
1 t vanilla

Mix ingredients for topping with a pastry blender or fingertips until butter is well incorporated. Set aside. Combine wet ingredients. Mix well. Add dry ingredients and mix until blended. Pour cake batter into an 8X8in square pan or 10in round pan. Sprinkle on topping and bake at 350° for 40-45 minutes.

Variation:

Peanut Butter Banana Coffee Cake: (Omit walnuts, applesauce, and nutmeg) Add 1 T peanut butter to topping. Add ½ cup peanut butter to wet and increase salt to ¾ t in dry.

CHOCOLATE COCONUT COFFEE CAKE

A decadent treat with an ooey gooey coconutty center. Mmmmmmm

Topping:
1/3 c ww flour
¼ c sugar
¼ c oatmeal
¼ c wide flake coconut
¼ c chocolate chips
2 T vegan butter or shortening
Cake:
2 c ww flour
2 ½ t baking powder

¾ t salt
1 c non-dairy milk
½ c sugar
¼ c oil
egg replacer equal to one egg
1 t vanilla
Center:
½ c each chocolate chips and wide flake
    coconut

Mix ingredients for topping with a pastry blender or fingertips until butter is well incorporated. Set aside. Combine wet ingredients and mix well. Add dry ingredients and mix until blended. Pour half of the batter into an 8X 8in square pan or 10in round pan. Evenly sprinkle on coconut then chocolate. Carefully pour on remaining batter. Sprinkle on topping and bake at 350° for 40-45 minutes until cake tester inserted in center comes out clean and coconut is not burned. Let cool for 10-15 minutes before serving.

CARROT COFFEE CAKE

Who knew you could have carrot cake for breakfast and feel good about it?

Topping:
1/3 c ww flour
¼ c sugar
¼ c oatmeal
¼ c walnuts
2 T vegan butter or shortening
½ t cinnamon
Cake:
2 c ww flour
2 ½ t baking powder
½ t cinnamon

½ t salt
¼ t each cloves, ginger, and nutmeg
1 c non-dairy milk
½ c sugar
¼ c applesauce
¼ c crushed pineapple
egg replacer equal to one egg
1 t vanilla
¾ c shredded carrot
½ c raisins

Soak raisins in hot water to cover. Mix ingredients for topping with a pastry blender or fingertips until butter is well incorporated. Set aside. Mix wet ingredients well except carrots and raisins. Drain raisins. Add carrot and raisins and mix briefly. Add dry ingredients and mix until just blended. Pour cake batter into an 8X8in square pan or 10in round pan. Sprinkle on topping and bake at 350° for 40-45 minutes until cake tester inserted in the center comes out clean. Let cool for 10-15 minutes before serving.

MAPLE ALMOND OAT COFFEE CAKE

All hail MAO the great communist leader of breakfast!

Topping:
1/3 c ww flour
¼ c sugar
¼ c oatmeal
¼ c raw whole almonds
2 T vegan butter or shortening
1 T maple syrup
½ t cinnamon
Cake:
1 c ww flour

1 c oatmeal
2 ½ t baking powder
½ t salt
½ t cinnamon
¾ c non-dairy milk
½ c maple syrup
¼ c applesauce
egg replacer equal to one egg
1 t vanilla
½ c chopped raw almonds

Mix ingredients for topping with a pastry blender or fingertips until butter is well incorporated. Set aside. Combine wet ingredients and mix well. Add dry ingredients and mix until blended. Pour cake batter into an 8X8in square pan or 10in round pan. Sprinkle on topping and bake at 350° for 40-45 minutes until cake tester inserted in the center comes out clean. Let cool for 10-15 minutes before serving.

COCOA SWIRL COFFEE CAKE

Chocolate for breakfast, what more could you want?

Swirl:
½ c sugar
¼ c cocoa powder
¼ c chocolate chips
3 T oil

Topping:
1/3 c ww flour
¼ c sugar
¼ c oatmeal
¼ c chocolate chips

2 T vegan butter or shortening

Cake:
2 c ww flour
2 ½ t baking powder
¾ t salt
1 c non-dairy milk
½ c sugar
¼ c oil
egg replacer equal to one egg
1 t vanilla

Mix ingredients for swirl until consistency of wet sand. Set aside. Mix ingredients for topping with a pastry blender or fingertips until butter is well incorporated. Set aside. Combine wet ingredients and mix well. Add dry ingredients and mix until blended. Add swirl to cake batter and fold until swirled. Pour cake batter into an 8X8in square pan or 10in round pan. Sprinkle on topping and bake at 350° for 40-45 minutes until cake tester inserted in the center comes out clean. Let cool for 10-15 minutes before serving. The center may sink a little while cooling, but do not despair, it is normal.

Variation:

Peanut Butter Cocoa Swirl Coffee Cake: Add 1 T peanut butter to topping and ½ c peanut butter to cake batter with wet ingredients. Prepare as above and prepare for nirvana.

MAY CONTAIN NUTS COFFEE CAKE

I named this for all of those fun allergy-warning labels. This not only may contain nuts, it is chock full of them!

Topping:
1/3 c ww flour
¼ c sugar
¼ c oatmeal
¼ c raw mixed nuts (I like almonds, cashews and walnuts)
2 T vegan butter or shortening
1 T nut butter
¼ t nutmeg

Cake:
2 c ww flour

2 ½ t baking powder
¾ t salt
½ t nutmeg
1 c non-dairy milk
½ c sugar
¼ oil (nut oil is great!)
2 T nut butter
egg replacer equal to one egg
1 T vanilla
½ c finely chopped raw mixed nuts

Mix ingredients for topping with a pastry blender or fingertips until butters are well incorporated. Set aside. Combine wet ingredients and mix well. Add dry ingredients and mix until blended. Pour cake batter into an 8X8in square pan or 10in round pan. Sprinkle on topping and bake at 350° for 40-45 minutes until cake tester inserted in the center comes out clean. Let cool for 10-15 minutes before serving.

PUMPKIN COFFEE CAKE

High in fiber, this moist breakfast treat is a great way to start your day with vitamin A!

Topping:
1/3 c ww flour
¼ c sugar
¼ c oatmeal
2 T vegan butter or shortening
½ t cinnamon

Cake:
2 c ww flour
2 ½ t baking powder

½ t salt
½ t cinnamon
¼ t each cloves, ginger, and nutmeg
1 c canned pumpkin
½ c non-dairy milk
½ c sugar
¼ c applesauce
egg replacer equal to one egg
1 t vanilla

Mix ingredients for topping with a pastry blender or fingertips until butter is well incorporated. Set aside. Combine wet ingredients and mix well. Add dry ingredients and mix until blended. Pour cake batter into an 8X8in square pan or 10in round pan. Sprinkle on topping and bake at 350° for 40-45 minutes until cake tester inserted in the center comes out clean. Let cool for 10-15 minutes before serving.

OATMEAL RAISIN COFFEE CAKE

Like a big slice o' oatmeal cookie.

Topping:
1/3 c ww flour
¼ c sugar
¼ c oatmeal
2 T vegan butter or shortening
½ t cinnamon

Cake:
1 c ww flour
1 c oatmeal
2 ½ t baking powder
½ t salt
½ t cinnamon
¼ t cloves
1 c non-dairy milk
½ c sugar
¼ c applesauce
egg replacer equal to one egg
1 t vanilla
½ c raisins

Soak raisins in hot water to cover. Mix ingredients for topping with a pastry blender or fingertips until butter is well incorporated. Set aside. Combine wet ingredients and mix well. Add dry ingredients and mix until blended. Drain raisins, add, and mix well. Pour cake batter into an 8X8in square pan or 10in round pan. Sprinkle on topping and bake at 350° for 40-45 minutes until cake tester inserted in the center comes out clean. Let cool for 10-15 minutes before serving.

Variation:

Oatmeal Chocolate Chip Coffee Cake: Replace raisins with chocolate chips and prepare as above and be prepared for rave reviews.

WHEAT FREE POUND CAKE

This pound cake is light and fluffy. It is whole grain, but tastes and looks like it's bad for you! You can make orange cranberry or lemon raspberry. Mmmmmm.

- 1 c non-hydrogenated shortening
- 1 c dry sweetener
- 1 t vanilla
- 1 t orange or lemon extract
- 1 T orange or lemon zest
- egg replacer equal to 4 eggs
- 1 c brown rice flour
- 1 c barley flour
- 1 t baking powder
- 1 c cranberries or raspberries

Optional Glaze:
- 1-2 T orange or lemon juice
- 1 c powdered sugar

Preheat oven to 325. Beat shortening on medium speed for 1 minute. Gradually add dry sweetener to shortening while beating. Beat until light and fluffy. Add vanilla, extract and zest.. Add egg replacer a little at a time, beating well after each addition. Scrape bowl often. Gradually add flours and baking powder, mixing on low. Fold in berries. Pour batter into a greased and floured loaf pan. Bake at 325 for 55-65 minutes. Cool on a wire rack for at least 10 minutes. If desired, drizzle a glaze over the top made from orange or lemon juice and powdered sugar.

CORNBREAD

This cornbread is perfect with World Famous Chili.

- 1 c flour
- 1 c cornbread
- ¼ c nutritional yeast
- 2 T dry sweetener
- 1 T baking powder
- ½ t salt
- 1 c non-dairy milk
- 2 T applesauce
- 2 T oil
- egg replacer equal to 2 eggs

Preheat oven to 425. Put dry ingredients in a bowl and combine well. Add wet ingredients and stir until well moistened. Put in a greased 8x8 pan. Bake for 15-20 minutes until a toothpick inserted in the center comes out clean.

I REMEMBER THOSE BISCUITS

These are memorable biscuits. Whenever my friend Jimi sees them he says, "I remember those!"

4c flour (white or whole wheat pastry)	*¼ c vegan butter*
8 t baking powder	*¼ c vegan shortening*
1/2 t baking soda	*2 c non-dairy milk*
1 1/2 t salt	*2 t vinegar*

Preheat oven to 425.

Pour vinegar into soymilk and let it sit while you prepare the dry ingredients.

Add all dry ingredients together in a large bowl. Mix well. Add vegan butter and shortening and mix together using your fingertips until all of the fat is combined with the dry ingredients and the mixture looks uniform. Stir in milk-vinegar mixture. Stir until "just mixed". Put dough on a well floured surface and dust with flour. Knead just a few times until dough is workable. Roll out dough and then cut out rounds. Place on cookie sheet and bake at 425 for 20 minutes, until golden brown on top.

Biscotti

ALMOND BISCOTTI

These crispy cookies are great with tea or coffee or dipped in chocolate.

3 c whole wheat pastry flour	Egg replacer equal to 3 eggs
1 T baking powder	1 t vanilla
½ t salt	1 t almond extract
½ c shortening	½ c chopped almonds
¾ c sugar	

Cream together shortening and sugar until well incorporated. Add egg replacer, beat well. Add extracts and mix well. Add dry ingredients and almonds. Mix until well incorporated. Should be the consistency of soft clay or play-doh but not sticky. Add water if mixture is too dry. Shape dough on a cookie sheet into a rectangle 5" X 9" X 1". Bake at 350°for 20 minutes. Remove from oven and let cool for 10 minutes on pan. Do not turn oven off. Slice into 1" pieces. Place cut side down on cookie sheet and bake for 10 minutes. Flip biscotti and cook for 10 more minutes. Biscotti should be lightly browned, crisp and tender. Let cool on wire rack before eating or dipping.

PUMPKIN HAZELNUT BISCOTTI

These fall treats are lower in fat than traditional biscotti, but just as special.

3 c whole wheat flour	Egg replacer equal to 3 eggs
1 T baking powder	1 t vanilla
½ t salt	½ c chopped hazelnuts
½ t cinnamon	**Topping:**
¼ t each cloves, ginger, and nutmeg	2 T canned pumpkin
½ c canned pumpkin	¼ c powdered sugar
¾ c sugar	non-dairy milk
2-4 T oil	¼ c chopped hazelnuts

Cream together pumpkin and sugar until well incorporated. Add egg replacer, beat well. Add vanilla and mix well. Add dry ingredients and hazelnuts. Mix until well incorporated. Should be the consistency of soft clay or play-doh but not sticky. Add water if mixture is too dry. Shape dough on a cookie sheet into a rectangle 5" X 9" X 1". Bake at 350°for 20 minutes. Remove from oven and let cool for 10 minutes on pan. Do not turn oven off. Slice into 1" pieces. Place cut side down on cookie sheet and bake for 10 minutes. Flip biscotti and cook for 10 more minutes. Biscotti should be lightly browned, crisp and tender. Let cool on wire rack for 10-20 minutes. For topping, mix pumpkin and powdered sugar well. Add non-dairy milk as needed to make a drizzling consistency. Drizzle glaze on cooled biscotti and top with chopped hazelnuts.

OATMEAL CHOCOLATE CHIP BISCOTTI

An Italian twist on an American classic.

1 ½ c whole wheat flour	*½ c shortening*
1 ½ oatmeal	*¾ c sugar*
1 T baking powder	*Egg replacer equal to 3 eggs*
½ salt	*1 t vanilla*
½ t cinnamon	*½ chocolate chips*
¼ t cloves	

Cream together shortening and sugar until well incorporated. Add egg replacer, beat well. Add vanilla and mix well. Add dry ingredients and chocolate chips. Mix until well incorporated. Should be the consistency of soft clay or play-doh but not sticky. Add water if mixture is too dry. Shape dough on a cookie sheet into a rectangle 5" X 9" X 1". Bake at 350°for 20 minutes. Remove from oven and let cool for 10 minutes on pan. Do not turn oven off. Slice into 1" pieces. Place cut side down on cookie sheet and bake for 10 minutes. Flip biscotti and cook for 10 more minutes. Biscotti should be lightly browned, crisp and tender. Let cool on wire rack before eating or dipping.

MOCHA ALMOND BISCOTTI

Yes, it is as good as it sounds!

3 c whole wheat flour	*Egg replacer equal to 3 eggs*
1 T baking powder	*¼ c strong brewed coffee*
1 T coffee grounds	*1 t vanilla*
½ t salt	*1 t almond extract*
½ c shortening	*½ c melted chocolate*
¾ c sugar	*¼ c chopped toasted almonds*

Cream together shortening and sugar until well incorporated. Add egg replacer, beat well. Add coffee and extracts and mix well. Add dry ingredients. Mix until well incorporated. Should be the consistency of soft clay or play-doh but not sticky. Add additional coffee if mixture is too dry. Shape dough on a cookie sheet into a rectangle 5" X 9" X 1". Bake at 350°for 20 minutes. Remove from oven and let cool for 10 minutes on pan. Do not turn oven off. Slice into 1" pieces. Place cut side down on cookie sheet and bake for 10 minutes. Flip biscotti and cook for 10 more minutes. Biscotti should be lightly browned, crisp and tender. Let cool for 10-20 minutes on a wire rack. Spread melted chocolate on one side of each biscotti and top with chopped almonds. Let cool and try not to eat the whole batch.

Dips and spreads

AS YOU LIKE IT HUMMUS

I love hummus! It confounds me how something so beige and bland looking can be such a taste sensation. Try it any which way but loose.

> *1 can garbanzo beans, drained*
> *2-3 cloves garlic*
> *Juice of 1 lemon*
> *3 T tahini*
>
> *¼ c. liquid of your choice (water, vegetable juice, olive oil, etc.)*
> *1 t salt*
> *½ t cumin (optional)*

For a variation add 1 c. of any of the following, or try different combinations:
Olives (black, green, kalamata)
Spinach
Carrot
Artichoke hearts
Roasted peppers
Fresh herbs
Sun dried tomatoes
Kale

Put all ingredients in a food processor and process until thick and creamy. Serve with a variety of items. Some of my favorites are pita, chips, crackers, pretzels, tortillas, French bread, veggies, apples, pears. The list goes on and on.

WHITE BEAN SPREAD

This spread is kind of like hummus' Italian cousin. It is great spread on crusty bread, or tortillas, or as the base for a great sandwich.

> *1 can white beans, drained*
> *1-2 cloves garlic*
> *Juice of 1 lemon*
>
> *½ t salt*
> *¼ t black pepper*

Put all ingredients in a food processor and process until almost smooth. Try not to eat it all en route to table.

BLACK BEAN HUMMUS

This hummus is a great twist on the original. Recent research suggest that darker beans like black beans are higher in vitamins and minerals. Eat up in good health!

- 1 can black beans, drained and rinsed
- 2 cloves garlic
- juice of 2 limes
- 2 T tahini
- 1 t salt
- ¼ t cumin
- ¼ t dried cilantro or 1 t fresh
- ¼ t paprika
- 1 T olive oil

Put all ingredients in a food processor and process until smooth. Serve with tortillas or flat bread and assorted veggies.

MAPLE MUSTARD BARBEQUE SAUCE

This sauce is perfect as a marinade for tofu.

- 1 c ketchup
- ½ c water
- ¼ c apple cider vinegar
- 2 T maple syrup
- 1 T onion powder
- 1 T Braggs
- 1 t prepared mustard (yellow, dijion, brown, deli)
- ¼ t mustard powder
- ¼ t garlic powder
- ¼ t salt
- dash hot sauce

Combine all ingredients in a saucepan and bring to a boil. Simmer for 10-15 minutes.

RED PEPPER CHEEZE DIP

This is Julie's favorite! It is raw!

- 1 c cashews, soaked overnight in water, then drained
- Juice of 1 lemon
- 1 clove garlic
- 1 red pepper, chopped
- 1 t salt
- ½ c water
- 1 t tumeric
- 1 t paprika

Put all ingredients in the blender and blend until very smooth. Serve with veggies or chips.

TEMPEH, MUSHROOM AND RED PEPPER PASTA TOPPER

This mix of sautéed goodness is a must for pasta or pizza.

4 cloves of garlic, minced
¼ c olive oil
5 mushrooms, chopped
½ package tempeh, diced
1 red pepper, sliced thinly
2 T green olives, diced
1 T soy sauce

1 t paprika
1 t salt
¼ t black pepper
1 T dried basil
¼ c parsley, chopped fine
½ c water or white wine

Heat a pan over medium heat. Add olive oil, garlic, mushrooms, tempeh, and red pepper. Cook over medium heat, stirring occasionally, until mushrooms and red peppers are soft and tempeh is browned. Add olives, soy sauce, paprika, salt, black pepper, basil and parsley. Stir well. Add water or wine and stir well. When water or wine is evaporated turn off heat and serve over pasta. Also a good topping for pizza.

SHAKE UP DRESSING FORMULA

I use this quick formula whenever I need salad dressing fast.

¼ c agave nectar
½ c apple cider vinegar
1 c olive oil
1 t salt
1 T dried herbs

1 t paprika
½ t mustard powder
¼ t cumin
¼ t black pepper

Put all ingredients in a bottle with a lid. Shake up and serve. Will keep in the fridge, just shake before serving.

Main Dishes

MUSHROOM RICE

This recipe is my rendition of a dish my mother used to make when we were growing up. Of course, she used good ole' Campbell's Cream of Mushroom™. I use a packaged vegan mushroom soup in this recipe, and it still tastes like what mom used to make!

4 c. water	1 carrot, diced
2 c. brown rice	¼ c. food yeast
2 c. creamy mushroom soup (vegan)	2 T Liquid Aminos
2 c. mushrooms, sliced	1 T salt
3 stalks celery, diced	¼ black pepper

Preheat oven to 375°

Combine all ingredients in a 13x9 pan. Cover tightly with foil. Bake for 1 ½ to 2 hours. Stir and check for seasoning during last half hour.

SUMMER'S SECRET SPAGHETTI

For years I could not make spaghetti sauce that was worth eating. After many a trial and error I came up with this method of doctoring up canned sauce. It is foolproof and delicious! Serve with Gorgeous Garlic Toast.

1 jar prepared spaghetti sauce (vegan)	1 T olive oil
1 c. sliced mushrooms	1 T maple syrup
1 c. spinach	1 T balsamic vinegar
1 onion, chopped	1 T oregano
3 cloves garlic, minced	1 T basil
1 carrot, grated	1 T dried parsley
1 zucchini, chopped	1 t chili powder
1 can chopped or stewed tomatoes	Salt and black pepper to taste
¼ c. red wine (optional)	1 lb favorite pasta

Heat water in large kettle to cook noodles. When boiling, add salt and noodles. Cook until al dente. Meanwhile, heat oil in large sauté pan. Sauté onion in oil until translucent. Add garlic and cook 1 minute. Add zucchini, carrot, and mushroom. Cook until mushrooms and zucchini are soft. Deglaze pan with red wine. Add herbs, spices, vinegar, and maple syrup. Bring to boil and cook until alcohol smell is gone. Add canned tomatoes and reduce until almost all liquid has evaporated. Add jar of prepared sauce. Let simmer for 5-10 minutes. Taste and adjust seasoning. Right before serving, add spinach and cook until wilted.

VEGANIZED BAKED PASTA

Originally, I found this recipe swimming in dairy. I liked the idea of not having to cook the pasta prior to baking. So, I "veganized" it! Now, fabulous baked pasta with only one dirty dish and little work. Yay!

1 jar prepared vegan pasta sauce
2 c. sliced or quartered mushrooms
1 ½ c. water
1 c. ground beef substitute (optional)
½ lb smallish pasta (ziti, rotini, penne, macaroni...)
1 carrot, grated
1 zucchini, diced

2 cloves garlic, minced
2 T dried herbs
1 T maple syrup
2 t salt
½ t black pepper
½ chili powder
vegan mozzarella

Preheat oven to 400°. Combine all ingredients except mozzarella in 13x9 pan. Cover with mozzarella. Cover with foil and bake for 55-60 minutes.

NOT CURRY

The night I made this recipe up as a quick dinner, my friend Dany said "it's like curry, but not spicy". So, it's Not Curry!

2 c quinoa, cooked
(heat 4 c salted water to boiling. Add quinoa and cook for about 20 minutes until tender and translucent. Drain excess water)
4 T olive oil
6 cloves garlic, chopped
2 green onions, sliced
8 mushrooms, chopped
1 zucchini, chopped
1 pkg of ground beef substitute

2 T tomato paste
1 t cumin
½ t paprika
½ t pepper
1 t salt
2 c water or beer
1 c spinach, chopped
¼ c nutritional yeast

Heat oil in sauce pan. Add garlic, green onion, mushrooms, zucchini, ground beef substitute, salt and pepper. Cook until vegetables are soft and ground beef substitute is firm. Add tomato paste and spices. Cook and stir for 2-5 minutes until tomato paste is well incorporated and spices are fragrant. Add liquid, spinach, and nutritional yeast and stir until spinach is wilted and all ingredients are well incorporated. Serve over quinoa.

LEMON GARLIC PASTA

This pasta dish is quick, easy, and delicious! Try it with a flavored pasta for an extra kick.

- 1 lb pasta cooked with ¼ c diced sundried tomatoes
- 4-6 cloves garlic, minced
- ¼ c olive oil
- 2 c spinach
- 1 t salt
- ½ t pepper
- ¼ diced black or kalamata olives
- ½ c nutritional yeast
- ¼ c vegan margarine
- juice of 2 lemons

Cook pasta with sundried tomatoes, drain and set aside. Heat oil and garlic in sauce pan. Cook until garlic is soft, but not brown. Add spinach, olives, salt, and pepper. Cook until spinach is wilted. Add nutritional yeast and margarine. Cook and stir until well combined and margarine is melted. Take off heat and add lemon juice and pasta with sundried tomatoes. Stir well and serve.

BLACK BEAN, RICE, AND KALE CASSEROLE

This easy Mexican inspired casserole would be great topped with fresh salsa and avocados.

- 1 c white rice
- 1 can black beans, drained and rinsed
- 2 c water or vegetable stock
- 2 cloves garlic, sliced
- 1 green onion, sliced
- 3 leaves kale, de-stemmed and chopped
- 2 T tomato paste
- ½ c frozen corn
- ¼ c sliced olives
- 2 ribs celery, sliced
- ¼ t black pepper
- 1 t salt
- ½ t cumin
- 1 t paprika
- ¼ t chili powder

Preheat oven to 375. Put all ingredients in a 13x9 pan. Stir well. Cover with foil and bake at 375 for 50-60 minutes. Top with shredded vegan cheese, if desired.

QUINOA MUSHROOM OVEN RISOTTO

This is THE simplest risotto recipe you will find. The result of baking the quinoa is a creamy, cheesy, easy main dish.

1 c quinoa, rinsed	*1 T total fresh sage, parsley, thyme minced*
1 c water or stock	*1 t salt*
1 c non-dairy milk	*½ t pepper*
1 c sliced mushrooms	*¼ t mustard powder*
½ c nutritional yeast	*¼ t onion powder*
2 cloves garlic, minced	*1 c sliced spinach*

Preheat oven to 375. Combine all ingredients except spinach in a 13x9 pan. Cover with foil and bake for 40 minutes. Add spinach, recover and bake for 5-10 minutes more until the quinoa is tender and the spinach is wilted. Top with freshly ground pepper and or freshly minced parsley.

CHEEZISH MACARONI

After much trial and error I finally have a mac and cheese recipe my kids and I love!

1 lb small pasta	*1 T lemon juice*
2 c water	*1 t tahini*
4 oz pimientos	*½ t onion powder*
¼ c nutritional yeast	*1 ½ salt*
¼ c quick oats	*few drops hot sauce*
2 T cornstarch	*¼ c vegan margarine*

Cook pasta in plenty of salted water according to package directions. Drain and set aside. Blend remaining ingredients except vegan margarine. When smooth, cook over medium heat whisking until smooth and thick. Add margarine, turn off heat, add noodles, stir and serve.

DIP

This has become a movie night staple in our house. It is quick and easy and great with chips (and beer)!

> 2 cans refried beans
> 1 can black beans, drained and rinsed
> 1 lb ground beef substitute
> 1 packet taco seasoning (or seasoning of
>   your choice)
>
> 1 onion, chopped
> 1 T oil
> 1 can olives, sliced
> 1 bell pepper, chopped
> 1 c shredded vegan cheese

Preheat oven to 375. Spread refried beans in a 13x9 in pan. Pour black beans on top and smooth out. Saute onion in oil until soft. Add beef substitute and taco seasoning and cook according to taco seasoning packet directions. Spread taco mixture on top of beans. Sprinkle olives on top. Sprinkle cheese on top. Cover with foil and cook for 20-30 minutes until warm all the way through and cheese is melted. Sprinkle bell pepper on top. Serve with chips, salsa, vegan sour cream, avocados/guacamole, tortillas…whatever you like.

TOFU PIRI PIRI

This recipe is based on a classic Argentinian dish. The tofu is marinaded in the spicy lemon herb Piri Piri sauce and then broiled or grilled. Serve with rice or potatoes. It can be very spicy if you add too many chili flakes, so be careful!

> **Piri Piri Marinade:**
> ¾ c lemon juice
> ¼ c lime juice
> ¾ c olive oil
> ¼ c minced garlic
> ½-2 t hot chili flakes
>
> 2 t dried oregano
> 1 t dried thyme
> 1 t cumin
> 1 t salt
> 1 lb tofu, pressed and sliced into 8 pieces
> 1 t cornstarch

Stir marinade ingredients together in a shallow dish. Marinade the tofu for at least 4 hours and up to 12 hours. Remove tofu from the marinade and broil or grill on each side for 5-10 minutes until browned and crisp. While the tofu is cooking, put the remaining marinade in a saucepan with the cornstarch. Wisk over medium high heat until thickened. Serve browned tofu with sauce.

SCRAMBLED TOFU

Not much is better than a lazy morning with Scrambled Tofu, Roasted Potatoes, Toast, and lots of Coffee!

2 T oil
1 lb firm tofu, drained
¼ c nutritional yeast
2 t salt
1 t black pepper
½ t paprika

¼ t tumeric
optional:
2 green onions, sliced
1 c spinach
1 c mushrooms, thinly sliced

Heat oil in skillet. Add all remaining ingredients. Stir while cooking over medium high heat. Cook until most of the liquid is evaporated and the tofu is a texture to your liking. Serve with roasted potatoes and toast. Eat way too much and lie around and moan.

FRUITED SWEET POTATOES

This recipe is an original take on baked sweet potatoes

4 sweet potatoes, peeled and sliced thick
1 apple, peeled and chopped
¼ c chopped dates
¼ c crushed pineapple
¼ c golden raisins
¼ c orange juice

¼ c pomegranate juice
1 T fresh ginger, finely grated
1 t salt
½ t cinnamon
¼ t nutmeg
¼ t pepper

Preheat oven to 350. Toss all ingredients in a 13x9 pan. Cover with foil and cook at 350 for 30-45 minutes, until potatoes are tender.

ROASTED ROOT VEGGIES

This is such a versatile recipe. You can use any mix of root veggies you like.

2 potatoes, scrubbed and chopped
2 sweet potatoes, peeled and chopped
2 carrots, scrubbed and chopped
2 beets, chopped

4 cloves garlic
2 T olive oil
1 t salt
½ t black pepper

Turn on broiler. Prep veggies and put on a cookie sheet with oil, salt, and pepper. When broiler is hot, put in veggies (about 6 in from broiler). Cook for 15 minutes. Stir and flip. Cook for 10-15 minutes more. Serve. This recipe can be made with any mix of root veggies you like. Beet, Carrot, Celeriac, Jerusalem Artichoke, Parsnip, Potato, Radish, Rutabaga, Sweet Potato, Turnip.

JOSEFINA-JOSEFINAS

After many trials I have come up with a great way to make jo-jo's at home.

4 potatoes, scrubbed and cut into wedges
1 T oil
½ t onion powder
¼ t cumin

¼ t chili powder
¼ t paprika
¼ t garlic powder

Preheat oven to 450. Mix all ingredients well on a sheet pan. Bake for 15 minutes. Flip, and bake for 10-15 more minutes. Let cool before eating.

ROASTED POTATOES

This simple recipe is just as good with Scrambled Tofu for breakfast as it is with veggie burgers for dinner. Mmmmm potatoes.

*1 potato for each person, washed and
  chopped
1-2 T oil for each potato
1 t salt for each potato*

*¼ t pepper for each potato
optional:
peeled garlic cloves*

Turn on broiler. Chop potato(es) and put on a sheet pan. Add oil, salt, and pepper and mix well with your hands. Put potatoes in oven and cook for 15 minutes. Turn potatoes and put on oven for 10-15 more minutes. Cool and eat waaaay too much.

ROASTED VEGGIES

Roasting is a quick and easy way to make a delicious vegetable dish. Some of my favorite vegetables to roast are asparagus and green beens. You could also prep veggies for roasting and throw them on the grill instead.

*1 lb veggies of your choice, sliced if needed
  such as: asparagus, brussel sprouts,
  cauliflower, green beans, mushrooms,
  sweet peppers, zucchini*

*1-2 T oil
1 t salt
½ t pepper*

Turn on broiler. Toss veggies with oil, salt, and pepper on sheet pan. Broil until veggies are tender, turning as needed.

SUCCOTASH

This side dish is a must for any southern feast.

> 1 can black eyed peas, drained and rinsed
> 1 can corn
> 4 c spinach, chopped
> ½ c vegan sausage, diced
>
> ¼ c salsa
> 2 T nutritional yeast
> 1 T oil
> ½ t salt

Saute sausage in oil until fragrant. Add spinach and toss until wilted. Add remaining ingredients and toss until warmed through. Serve with "I remember those Biscuits".

GORGEOUS GARLIC TOAST

After many trials, my family deemed this one a winner. Your friends and guests will agree that this is impossible to resist!

> 1 large loaf French, Italian, or
>   Sourdough Bread, sliced thick
> ½ c. vegan butter
>
> 4 cloves garlic, minced
> 2 T food yeast
> ½ t salt

Preheat broiler. Mix "butter", garlic, food yeast, and salt. Spread on bread. Place directly on rack in oven 3-6 inches from broiler. Toast under broiler for 2-5 minutes until golden brown and delicious. If there is any "butter" mix left, add to spaghetti sauce right before serving. Delicioso!

Soups and salads

TOO HOT TO COOK QUINOA SALAD

During the summer I just can't bear standing over a hot stove, cooking. Quick cooking quinoa to the rescue! Quinoa cooks in 15-20 minutes and is high in protein. A great base for cold salad in the summer! Be sure to rinse the quinoa under cold water before cooking. This rinses off a bitter residue called saponin, which is quinoa's own natural insect repellant.

Salad:
2 c. cooked and cooled quinoa
2 c. spinach
1 head romaine, chopped or torn
1 c. frozen peas, thawed
1 cucumber, diced
1 can garbanzo beans, drained & rinsed
1 rib celery, diced

1 yellow bell pepper, sliced thin
1 c. green beans, cut in 1 in. lengths,
   blanched and cooled

Dressing:
¾ c. olive oil
zest and juice of 1 lemon
salt & black pepper to taste

Combine salad ingredients in a bowl. In a jar, combine dressing ingredients and shake well. Pour dressing over salad, toss, and serve. Serve with hummus, pitas or tortillas, and tofu feta.

TRIPLE CITRUS SPINACH SALAD

This salad is the perfect accompaniment to any savory entrée, such as mushroom rice. It is also great as on its own as a light meal or snack.

Salad:
2 c. baby spinach leaves
1 grapefruit
1 blood orange
1 small can mandarin oranges, drained
¼ c. cashews, toasted & chopped

Dressing:
Juice from citrus
2 T olive oil
1 t maple syrup
½ t salt
¼ t black pepper

Section grapefruit and blood orange over a bowl, reserving juice. Put citrus sections in a salad bowl with remaining salad ingredients. Combine dressing ingredients in a jar and shake to combine. Pour over salad, toss, and serve

SIMON'S RED & GREEN SOUP

My son Simon's favorite colors are red and green. In an effort to convince him to try tomato soup, I invented this special homage to his favorite colors. And he eats it, too!

2 c. tomato soup (vegan)	1 tomato, diced
1 c. couscous, raw	½ c. frozen peas
1 c. spinach, chopped	½ c. cooked beets
1 green bell pepper	¼ c. chopped parsley
1 red bell pepper	

Prepare couscous according to package directions. Heat soup with any combination of red and green vegetables. To serve, mound large spoonful of couscous in bowl, and add soup to cover.

WORLD FAMOUS CHILI

For a short time I made this chili at a local café. It got rave reviews! Make it for your friends and you can get raves too!

2 T oil	2 cans chopped tomato
2 onion, chopped	¼ c refried beans
2 red pepper, chopped	½ t salt
2 carrots, shredded	½ t pepper
4 cloves garlic, minced	¾ t cumin
2 cans beans, any kind, drained and rinsed	½ t oregano
	½-2 t chili powder

Saute onion in oil over medium heat. Cover and cook for 5-10 minutes until soft. Add garlic, peppers, and carrots. Cover and cook for 10-15 minutes. Add tomatoes, spices, and canned beans and cook uncovered for 15-20 minutes. Add refried beans and stir until well combined and thickened. Serve with cornbread.

ISRAELI COUS COUS SALAD WITH CARROT VINAIGRETTE

Israeli cous cous is much larger than ordinary cous cous. The pearls are the size of peas. This salad really makes the most of its wonderful texture.

2 c dry Israeli cous cous, cooked and
   cooled to room temperature
2 ribs celery, diced
1 bell pepper, halved
1 can mandarin oranges
1 small yellow zucchini, diced
1 small green zucchini, diced
1 c chicken flavored seitan, diced

¼ c chopped olives
2 sundried tomatoes, minced
Vinaigrette:
¾ c fresh carrot juice
¼ c balsamic vinegar
½-1 c olive oil
salt and black pepper to taste

Roast diced zucchini and one half of bell pepper under the broiler until well browned. Set aside to cool. Peel and dice roasted pepper. Dice other half of pepper. Toss together all ingredients. Put vinaigrette ingredients in a jar and shake until well combined. Pour over salad and serve at room temperature.

ROAD TRIP QUINOA SALAD

I made this salad for our first vegan road trip and it kept us satisfied. It is perfect for a road trip because it gets better the longer it sits. Just be sure to keep it in a cooler!

2 c quinoa, cooked and cooled
3 multi-colored peppers, roasted, peeled
   and chopped
1 c garbanzo beans, drained and rinsed
5 sundried tomatoes
1 c cooked and cooled rainbow orzo
1 rib celery, diced

¼ c sliced olives
1 c chopped spinach
1/3 c lemon juice
2/3 c olive oil
1 T red wine vinegar
2 T soy sauce
1 t pepper

Toss together salad ingredients. Shake dressing ingredients in a small jar. Pour dressing over salad and toss. Let sit covered in the refrigerator over night.

MANGO & RUNNER BEAN SALAD

Runner beans are a variety of heirloom bean. You should be able to find them canned at your local natural food store. If you are unable to find them you can substitute kidney beans.

Salad:
2 mangos, diced
1 cucumber, diced
2 ribs celery, diced
½ bell pepper, diced
1 carrot, shredded
2 c spinach, chopped
1 can runner beans, drained and rinsed
¼ c silken tofu, drained and crumbled

Dressing;
juice of ½ lemon
2 t salt
1 tsp maple syrup
1 t red wine vinegar
1 t Dijon mustard
¼ t pepper
olive oil as needed (¼ - ½ c)

Combine salad ingredients. Put dressing ingredients in a blender. Run on low and drizzle in oil until lemony colored and creamy. Toss salad with dressing and serve.

PASTA SALAD

My son loves this salad. Good source of protein and fat for his growing body!

1 lb small pasta
cooked with
2 sundried tomatoes, diced
drain, rinse in cold water and set aside
In bowl, mix
1 collard green leaf, thinly sliced
1 carrot, shredded
1 green onion, thinly sliced
1 c green peas

1 c protein of choice (seitan, tofu, tempeh, etc)
1/3 c vegan mayonnaise
¼ c nutritional yeast
2 T apple cider vinegar
1 T prepared mustard
1 T soy sauce
¼ t pepper

Mix well, add pasta and tomatoes and mix again. Serve cold.

CROCKPOT BEAN SOUP

There is nothing easier than soup in the crockpot. This is the easiest bean soup recipe, and it's tasty, too! You can use any kind or mix of beans that you desire.

Soak overnight
2 c dried beans of your choice (use one kind or a mix, whatever you have)

After soaking, drain and rinse. Put in crockpot and cover with water. Add

1 onion, chopped
4 cloves garlic, minced
2 collard leaves, thinly sliced
1 T kelp flakes (optional)
cook on low until beans are tender. Add
1 15 oz can diced tomatoes or 6 oz can
*   tomato paste*

1 c frozen corn
1-3 T dried herbs of your choice
2-4 t salt
1 t black pepper
1 t molasses

Let cook until warmed through, then serve.

BLUEPRINT FOR A KICK ASS GREEN SALAD

Since my husband became a raw foodist, I have perfected my awesome green salad. This is what my husband has for lunch most days. Let me tell you, salad is not boring! Try it!

Serves 1 for a meal, or 2-4 as a side dish

Combine the following in a bowl with a lid.

1 kind lettuce (romaine, green leaf,
*   butter) chopped or shredded*
2 kinds greens/cabbage (kale, swiss chard,
*   spinach, purple cabbage, savoy cabbage)*
*   chopped, shredded, or julliened*
2 kinds non-sweet fruit (cucumber,
*   zucchini, tomato, bell pepper) diced or*
*   julienned*

2 kinds vegetable (jicama, carrot, celery,
*   beet, broccoli, cauliflower) diced or*
*   julienned*
1 or 2 kinds nut or seed, chopped if
*   necessary*

optional:
sprouts (quinoa, alfalfa, bean, pea), sweet
*   fruit (apple, pear, dried cranberries,*
*   strawberries) diced, protein (smoked*
*   tofu, veggie bacon, canned beans)*

Pour dressing over top, put lid on and shake it! Eat. Lots.

MY FAVORITE LENTIL SOUP

I love lentils! And I love this soup! It cooks in less than an hour and is very nice on cold days.

Heat soup pan. Add

1 T olive oil
1 onion, chopped
2 cloves garlic, minced
cook until onion and garlic are soft, but
   not brown. Add
1 c dry lentils, rinsed
4 cups veggie broth or water

1 can diced tomatoes
1 T soy sauce
¼ t dried thyme
¼ t pepper
¼ t ground cumin
1 bay leaf

Bring to a boil. Reduce heat, cover, and simmer for 15 minutes. Add
1 carrot, diced
2 stalks celery, diced
1 c veggie sausage

Return to boiling, reduce to a simmer and cook uncovered for 15-20 minutes, until lentils and veggies are tender. Get bay leaf out of pot before serving.

FALL CROCKPOT SOUP

1 onion, chopped
5 cloves garlic, minced
1 carrot, chopped
2 ribs celery, chopped
1 c corn
2 small yellow squash, chopped
2 collard leaves, sliced
1 c lentils

½ c brown rice
¼ c parsley, chopped
6 c water
2 t cumin
2 t paprika
1 t curry
1 t dried herbs
½ t black pepper

Put all ingredients in crock pot and cook on low heat for 6-8 hours. When lentils and rice are done, add:
2 t salt
2 T tomato paste
1 c water

Continue to heat until warmed through and serve.

Sweets

CHOCOLATE ALMOND COOKIES

These cookies are dangerous. Do not allow yourself alone with these unless you intend to eat them all!

½ c shortening
¾ c sugar
egg replacer equal to one egg
½ t vanilla extract
½ t almond extract
1/3 c chopped almonds

3 T soymilk
2/3 c flour
1/3 c cocoa powder
1/3 c quick oats
1/8 t baking soda
1/8 t salt

Preheat oven to 375. Beat together shortening, sugar, egg replacer, extracts, almonds, and soymilk until well combined and fluffy. Add dry ingredients and beat well. Drop rounded spoonfuls on to sheet pans and bake for 8-10 minutes. Cool and eat.

GGB'S OATMEAL RAISIN COOKIES

These cookies are the ones that were always available in my Grandma Betty's black cat cookie jar. I knew that I had to veganize these and continue the tradition. My kids call her GGB, short for Great Grandma Betty.

½ c shortening
1 ¼ c sugar
egg replacer equal to 2 eggs
6 T molasses
1 ¾ c flour
1 t baking soda

1 t salt
1 t cinnamon
2 c rolled oats
1 c raisins
½ c walnuts, chopped fine

Preheat oven to 400. Cream together shortening, sugar, egg replacer, and molasses. Sift and stir in flour, soda, salt, and cinnamon. Stir in oats, raisins, and walnuts. Drop rounded spoonfuls about 2" apart on sheet pans. Bake for 5-8 minutes until lightly browned. Cool and eat!

OATMEAL CHOCOLATE CHIP WALNUT COOKIES

Dennis Kucinich has eaten this cookie!

½ c shortening
¾ c sugar
egg replacer equal to one egg
3 T soymilk
1 T molasses
1 t vanilla extract
1 c flour

2/3 c oats
½ c chocolate chips
1/3 c walnuts
1/8 t cinnamon
1/8 t salt
1/8 t baking soda

Preheat oven to 375. Cream together shortening, sugar, egg replacer, soymilk, molasses, and vanilla. Add the rest of the ingredients and mix well. Drop by rounded spoonfuls on to sheet pans and bake for 10-15 minutes until lightly browned.

WHEAT FREE CHOCOLATE CHIP COOKIES

These cookies are wheat free, but do contain gluten. They are also nut and soy free. Oh yeah, and they are delicious!

½ c shortening
¾ c sugar
2 T flax meal
3 T water
3 T rice milk
½ t vanilla extract

1 c barley flour
1 c brown rice flour
1 t baking powder
¼ t salt
½ c chocolate chips

Preheat oven to 375. Cream together shortening, dry sweetener, flax meal, water, rice milk, and vanilla extract. Add remaining ingredients and mix well. Drop by rounded spoonfuls onto sheet pans. Bake for 10-15 minutes until lightly browned.

WHEAT FREE OATMEAL COOKIES WITH RAISIN OR GINGER

These cookies are wheat free but not gluten free. They are also nut and soy free. Yum yum! Try the ginger variation, it's fab!

½ c shortening	1 ¼ c rolled oats
¾ c sugar	1 c barley flour
2 T flax meal	1 t baking powder
3 T water	½ t cinnamon
3 T rice milk	½ t cloves or ginger
1 t molasses	¼ t salt
¼ t vanilla	½ c raisins or candied ginger

Preheat oven to 375. Cream together shortening, sugar, flax meal, water, rice milk, molasses, and vanilla. Add the remaining ingredients and mix well. Drop by rounded spoonfuls on a sheet pan. Bake for 10-15 minutes until lightly browned. Cool and eat.

CARAMEL

It is incredibly easy to make your own dairy-free caramel. The only special equipment needed is a candy thermometer.

1 c margarine	1 c light corn syrup
2 c sugar	1 t vanilla
2 c full fat soymilk	

Line a square pan with foil. Spread some margarine on the foil. Set aside.

In a 3 qt sauce pan, melt margarine over medium heat. Add all remaining ingredients except the vanilla. Stir over medium heat until boiling. Put candy thermometer in pan. Continue to cook over medium or medium low heat until candy thermometer reads 248 (firm ball stage).

Remove from heat and take thermometer out of pan. Add vanilla. Pour caramel into prepared pan. Let cool until firm.

Add-Ins:

Sprinkle nuts in the bottom of the prepared pan before adding caramel
Sprinkle chocolate chips on the caramel after pouring it into the pan. The heat of the caramel will melt the chocolate, and then you can spread it evenly.

BRITTLE

This brittle is great with any nut or seed you would like to add. This is also a great topping for biscotti.

2 c sugar
1 c light corn syrup
¼ c margarine

½ c water
2 c nuts or seeds of choice
1 ½ t baking soda

Spread margarine on two sheet pans and set aside. In a saucepan combine sugar, corn syrup, margarine, and water. Cook and stir over medium high heat until boiling. Put candy thermometer in pan. Cook and stir over medium heat to 275 (soft crack stage). Add nuts, and heat to 295 (hard crack stage). Remove saucepan from heat and remove thermometer from pan. Sprinkle soda over mixture and stir well. Pour into prepared baking sheets. Cool and break into pieces.

MANGO WITH SWEET YOUNG COCONUT SAUCE

I created this raw dessert for my husband. It is reminiscent of mango and sticky rice.

2 mangos, peeled and julienned or
    shredded
1 young coconut

2 T agave nectar
½ t vanilla extract
pinch of salt

Put mango in a bowl.

Open young coconut and reserve coconut water. Spoon out meat of the coconut and put it a blender. Add the agave, vanilla, salt, and ¼ cup of coconut water. Blend until smooth. Add more coconut water if you want the sauce to be thinner.

Pour sauce over the mango and serve.

THE BROWNIES THAT WERE ALMOST LOST

I went on a quest to come up with a fudgey vegan brownie. I spent time off and on for a year developing a recipe. After many failed attempts, I finally got THE recipe. And then I forgot to write it down. And I forgot the recipe. While finishing up this book I went back to the kitchen to revive the recipe. Luckily, it didn't take me a year to figure out the recipe again!

> 4 oz unsweetened baking chocolate
> ½ c vegan margarine
> ½ c silken tofu
> 2 T flax seed
> 3 T agar
> ½ c water
>
> 2 c sugar
> 1 t vanilla extract
> 1 c flour
> 1 t baking powder
> ½ t salt

Preheat oven to 350. Grease and flour a 13X9 inch pan.

Over simmering water, melt chocolate and margarine. Set aside to cool.

Pour ¼ water into a pan. Add agar. Stir and heat until agar dissolves.

In a blender, finely grind flax seed. Add tofu and agar-water mixture and blend until smooth. Pour into a bowl and mix on medium speed while adding sugar slowly. Add in vanilla. Fold in chocolate/margarine mixture. Fold in flour, baking powder, and salt. Pour into prepared pan. Bake for 25-30 minutes. Let cool.

MIRACLE CREAMY COCONUT FIRST TRY PIE

This pie must have been meant to be, because this experimental recipe worked on the first try!

> 1 lb silken tofu
> 1 16 oz can coconut milk
> ¾ c sugar
> ¼ c cornstarch
> 1 t vanilla
>
> ¼ t salt
> Egg replacer 1 egg
> ¾ c shredded coconut
> 1 crust

Preheat oven to 375.

Put everything except for the crust and the coconut in a food processor or blender and blend until very smooth. Stir in coconut and pour into the crust. Bake for 1 hour. Filling will not be firm, but with thicken as it cools. Serve cold or at room temperature.